RAMBLINGS OF A WARPED MIND

RAMBLINGS OF A WARPED MIND

RODNEY JOHNSON

ISBN-13: 9780692954959
ISBN-10: 0692954953

Dedicated to my granddaughter Anna Jane

This is a collection of Poetry and a few short stories that I wrote in my 20's (I am in my 70's now). They would have probably stayed ignored and forgotten, except my granddaughter had one of her short stories published and this made me decide to have mine published even if I had to pay for it and I did.

Most of my poems scream with emotion, so I am going start off with a poem that has no strong emotion, only tranquility. It had no title, so I gave it one. The first one I thought of was "Moonlit Beach", but I choose:

CALIFORNIA

Walk out of the mist filled cave
Walk down to the shifting sand
that is the shore
Listen to the roar of the earthbound sea
While you bask in the reflected light
from a hidden sun
Let the titanic voice of the sea
cleanse your mind
and free your senses
Let your eyes gaze upon all
that the heavens contain
Move your fingers through the sand
The harsh coarseness of the small
smooth grains of sand.

The next one also had no title, but I am going to leave it that way, but is one that I can always remember and one I enjoy saying out loud

A hand is all that's left
Reaching out of the blood red sea
It cries and moans for help
Help that can never be.

This next one I didn't know what to do about it. I lost the first page and I have no idea how to recreate it. I don't even remember the title or even if I had one, so I am just going to put here what I still have, just remember the first part is missing. I am going to call what I have left of the poem –

CRAZY

can't be true
and then the truth begins to creep in
from some dark corner of the brain
dazed
But the coil spring begins to
tighten
faster
faster and faster the coil spring tightens
run
run, howl, scream, cry, sob, moan
scream the demented cry of a mind gone
mad
howl the hopeless pitiful wail
of a dog with a turpentined ass
sob
sob hysterically until the mouth begins to foam
crawl with your head between your legs
looking for some dark rock to hide under
but the tightening of the coil spring
slows
the writhing spasms cease

things slowly begin to go back to
normal
but the coil spring still tightens
and a certain part of the brain
begins to deteriorate
The dark unknown looms ahead.

This next one is the only political one.

THE GREAT TREATISE

There are but two forms of government
The hard and the soft
Most governments today are blends of the two
but we (U.S.) are on a rocket heading straight
to the really HARD.

On this one I have revised on the title, but I don't remember revising it, but I must have right after I finished it the first time. I have no idea what I changed.

TIME (REVISED)

Time is the essence
Time is the all important
Time is silent
Time is colorless
Time is unnoticeable
indefinitely and infinitely
Time is endless
Time is old –
infinitely and incredibly
Eons of time have passed
And yet, time has no age
Time is no age
Time was no age
And yet again
Time has not changed
Time is not changed
Time will not change
Time can not change
      -For time is time-

One of the themes in several of my poems, including this one, is that after you die and when last of the few people that really knew you die, every trace of you is gone except for genetics. I think this is true even of famous people, for example, Thomas Jefferson, who is said to have loved his wife so much that, after she died young after childbirth, he never looked at another woman; but the truth is that shortly after her death, he started sleeping with a slave, his wife's much, much younger half-sister and stayed with her for the rest of his life. Who really knows who the real Thomas Jefferson was? Who really knows the person they are married to? I think many of us don't.

THE SPIDER

Each man is a spider unto himself
Spinning his own little web
Eagerly awaiting
The vibrations
Of another's touch
Waiting
And waiting
While the cobweb gathers dust
Hungry
So very hungry
Starving for the touch
That will never come
Till death shrivels
The spider to dust

THE TEMPORARY MAN

I am a temporary man
a moment after I am gone
there is no trace that I have been
as I walk along in sand
my footsteps disappear behind me

I am a temporary man
When I talk to people who used
to be part of my life
their memories are not my memories
I have went back to where
I have been before
and there is nothing there
left of me

I am a temporary man
I have left no mark
And so it will be when I die
I will leave no sign
to show that I existed for a moment
and neither will you

This next one I wrote when I was in a good mood. It is just the way I first wrote it. I did not even give it much thought. I think it is pretty funny.

GOD

I am God
I live in an insane asylum
You doubt that God needs
to be in an insane asylum?
Look at yourself
I made you
Now do you doubt that God
Belongs in an insane asylum?

This next one I wrote when I was feeling sorry for myself. I don't think it is very good and I think most of us deserve what we get in life most of the time.

PAIN TIME

What's left of a man
when the woman he's loved
for so many years
tells him she doesn't love him
and never did?
What's left of a man
when the woman he's loved
for so-o many years
tells him she loves
Someone else?

What's left of a man
when the woman he's loved
for so-o-o many years
tells him that she is dying
for someone else's body?
What's left of a man
when the woman he's loved
for so-o-o many years
tells him that the only way

she can have sex with him
is to think of someone else?
Oh God, yes, Whats left of a man?
Nothing?
There was no man to begin with.

Something I scribbled on a napkin

THE SAHARA (4,000 YRS. AGO)

We were once the brave
We were the first out of the cave
We were happy, proud, and strong
Now all that's left is an ageless song
Where there were once green pastures
That animals use to roam
Now all that's left is the drifting sand.

It's so hot and dry
Another month has past
still no rain
the grass is brown
more people go forth
following the herds north
fewer and fewer animals
the rivers so low
stagnant, muddy water
the women weep
the children cry
I wonder how long
This drought will last

The waters seep
Into the ground
Where once mighty rivers
used to flow
now all that's left is the sand
that endless winds blow

This is my drinking poem. When I drink alone I am often pleasantly melancholy. I know those two words do not go together, but it is a difficult feeling to describe and these two words come the closest. This poem is basically what I do during that time.

SADNESS

Sadness for the things
that would have been.
but could not be
and sadness for the things
that almost were
but sadness most of all
for the things that ought to be
but never will

This is my favorite poem.

INEZ AND I

Warm together in bed
bathed in blue light
Moving slowly
Together with rhythm
For hours
while the record player
plays
soft, sad – sweet soul
And I wish it would
last forever

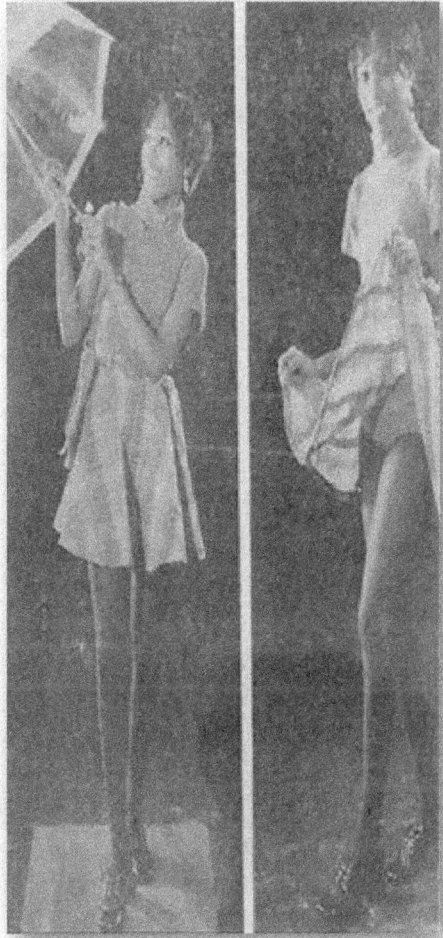

I have always tried to take the easy way in life, but at the same time stay true to myself. I am a good decent person, but unfortunately I tend to be a little cool and distant, like my mother was – God rest her soul. I loved her so much.

DROWN

Drown,
Drown in an ocean of thought
Float, float in a swift vast current
A current of pure ecstatic meditation
Sink, sink into deep dark cold
the bitter cold of a vast sea
The sea of the mass – the unsavable
Do not struggle, do not try to rise
It is a long way to the top of the wave

I was 27 years old when I wrote that and I am 76 years old now
and I still feel the same way. Just substitute 76 for the 27.

27

Only 27 years
and yet so many tears
for the moment
that's gone by
in the blink of an eye.
My life is bent
by the way
my day has went
and so every year
I drink more beer
And the time goes that much quicker
like a candle lights flicker
while I get a little more sicker

I exaggerate a little (lol) in this poem, but basically it could be about any woman I have loved.

DREAM

I once knew a girl who used to
die a thousand deaths when I was
late and who used to be content
just to be near me

     I once knew a girl ....
          She used to dream dreams with me
I once knew a girl who use to
Tremble at my touch and cry out
In ecstasy when we made love

     I once knew a girl ....
          She used to dream dreams with me

I once knew a girl who used to
scream and rage in the night if I
looked at someone else and who used
to be satisfied just to know I cared

     I once knew a girl ....
          She used to dream dreams with me

I once knew a girl who desperately
wanted to go anywhere I went and
who used to love being with me

I once knew a girl ….
But now another person knows her

I went up to the top of Mt. Evans (over 14,000 ft. high) when I was 19 and ran around like a kid, even climbing way out on the highest rock over hang and looking thousands of feet straight down. It was so exciting, everyone else was walking very slow and stopping to breath, someone was even using the emergency oxygen tanks; but It was so normal for me, almost like I was born to be there.

I went back there more than 20 years later and felt exactly the same way. I was with a group of men and they were all struggling, but not me. I was 19 again.

ROCKY MOUNTAINS

The meter sits in every brain
gauging, judging just what type
of thing you are
The brain is a vast complex thing
of dead pale white worms
and a powerful potential
of pure energy
A man stands
no higher than his will
no lower than a shrew
The sum of all life
is no greater than a jellyfish

Today I saw the Rockies for the first time
They created a very strong death urge
within me
To climb up, up so high
to the top of the earth
to the middle of the sky
and then, after you have reached the very top
reach for the burning sun
walk off into the sky
Live before you die

GOODBYE

Will you ever forgive me, dear
for running out on you this way
Will you listen to me dear?
While I tell you about the day
that we met on the top of Pine Hill
in the sweet spring of May

Can you remember the day too, dear?
The soft dry pine needles,
the sweet scents of a spring day
The comforting warmth
of that single sun ray
and the way you and I
loved one another

I'm sorry, dear, but there's
no reason, no rhyme
for leaving you after such
a short time

Do not worry, dear
for I do not fear
the darkness
and please do not cry
because I'm leaving you this way
just remember the day
that we met on a hill far, away

MIRROR

I must go to the end of this land
where there is a mirror on a wall
put there by my hand
and I never want it to fall

I must go to the end of this land
Where the deep blue sea
meets the soft white sand
and where my love waits for me

I must go
Like the river must flow
And the wind must blow
I must go to the end of the land

THE MAN

I'm as much of a man
as a man can be
without raping every
woman I see

I let my hair grow
long and soft on my head
and I love to wear
silk pajamas to bed

but still
I'm as much of a man
as a man can be
without trying to make
every woman I see
I hate to hunt
I don't like to fish
Really, I'd much rather
Look at clothes and wish

Yet I'm as much of a man
as a man can be
without making everyone
subservient to me.

SHARLIE

I remember when
You wanted a cup
You washed it

A time was when
kids cried
and people sighed
but Sharlie didn't care
"let the people stare"

When people were sad
and things got bad
Sharlie would take a walk
"let the people talk"

Sharlie loved to hate

TRUE

Such a fantastic angel
that I knew it could not be
No such beautiful angel
would ever speak to me
But once again
the angel said, "hello"
I didn't know what to do
So, knowing I was dreaming
and yet half believing
I said to myself
maybe it could be true
maybe an angel could
say hello to you

PITY

Oh God in the heavens above
If you really are
Then why?
Oh, why did I have to die?
If you really are
Why couldn't you
Why wouldn't you
Let me live
A long while ago
when I was younger
and first started to die
Why didn't you do something?
Why did you pass me by?
Oh God, if you really are
why did you even let me?
start to die
What great master plan of yours
was more important
than my life?
Oh God, what huge fantastic
master plan of yours was so important
that for it, I had to die?
Every time I go someplace to cry
oh God, I always wonder why
did I have to die?

I am very proud of this poem. I put some work into it.

LOST LOVE

Long ago, when I was very young
my love and I
built shining sand castles in the sun
She would build one half and I the other
we would build together
until it was done
and then one day she was gone
she swam out to far into the sea
The very next day I walked away
to the spot where she had left the land
I wanted to be, able to see, whether or not
she would return to me
but all I saw was sea and sand
I raised my head unto the sky
to choke back the tears
but I couldn't, I had to cry
I built a half of a sand castle
on the beach
close to the sea, within its reach
I stepped back and cried into the wind
That came from the sea
"Finish the sand castle, please, for me"
I stood and watched the waves
from the ocean, cover the castle
until there was nothing left to see

I went away from my home and the sea
I lived my life
and then I met another
and made her my wife
Back home went I to show everyone
my new bride
While there I grew restless
And we went for a ride
I drove to the sea
Where once long ago
my love had left me
as I drove along
an old man shouted at me
"A body's come up to shore", said he
I left the car and ran to the sea
I knew there she would be
She had floated up from the depths
drifted in from the sea
and next to the body
half of a sand castle waited for me
I knelt in the sand and finished the castle
For her, you see
And then I walked back to the car
where a stranger waited for me.

During this time that I was writing, Ray Bradbury was my favorite author. One day I was daydreaming, like I often did and still do, and this vision of sailboats gliding across a desert came to me. I wrote this poem based on that vision. I did not get it from the book or anywhere else. It was only 40 yrs. Later that It made me think of his book.

This poem is a dedication to the book "Martian Chronicles" written by the late great, Ray Bradbury

MARS

The blue boats sail with the wind
across the barren sea of sand
Driven by a whispering wind
they glide across the silent land
Each sailed by a being
with a silent mask upon his face
Living past their time
they are the last of a dying race
Drifting across the twilight desert floor
dying with majestic dignity
not with a feeble discontented roar
They are the last, the very end
for after them there will be no more

SHORT STORIES SECTION

The next two are Fiction and X rated

SCOTCH ON THE ROCKS

"Oh, Christ Phil, have I got something to tell you" Let's go get a drink, boy have I got a story to tell you" God, you won't believe it, I can hardly believe it myself.

Hey bartender, two scotch on the rocks, 'Old Parr' if you have it, if not the house scotch is fine.

Wait 'll I tell you what happened to me.

Jesus, this drink hits the spot.

I was talking to this girl at work and she mentioned she needed a ride and so I asked where to and since it wasn't to far away. I said I would. Hey now, I had no idea anything would happen, because I just don't go around making passes, too scared I guess, and besides this girl is the most devastating black girl you ever saw, all beautiful long slender legs. Well anyway I stopped in front of her place and she said she didn't feel like calling it quits yet and would I mind taking her for a ride first.

Bartender, two more scotches.

So, I started driving again. Now I am pretty dumb some-times, but the idea did enter my mind about time that maybe she wanted me. But, the lousy coward that I am I need it spelled out for me, so I asked her if she had anyplace particular in mind that she wanted to go and she said "look do I have to lead by the hand. So, I just keep driving away from the city, now I don't know any place to park, you know I've only been here a few months, but I drove until I found a likely looking spot an empty company parking lot with very little light. I stopped the car freezing cold out, but I was low on gas so I couldn't leave it running. I never saw two people get in the back seat and get their clothes off as quick as we did. You won't believe this but all the time I was looking for a place to park I was worried that I'd be lousy at it and hit it right away leaving her all unsatisfied and so you know what I don't even get excited, there I am laying with this fabulous black body with small beautiful breast and I don't even get excited. We just lay there for a while kissing, holding and touching until I finally get excited, she gets on top and puts it in and we move quiet and slow until we switch positions and then I speed up the tempo trying to come, she comes again and again but not me. We lay there freezing until finally I give up. While I am driving her home, she tells me that I seemed different the rest of the guys at work. She had wanted to do this with me and that whenever she thinks about something hard enough it always comes true. I tell her she is a beautiful witch and has cast a spell on me

Bartender, two more scotches

What? What did you say Phil? Why did I do it? Christ, what a stupid question. What man wouldn't if he had the chance.

Well ......

Well if you really want to know the truth. I've been feeling really depressed for some time. My wife loves some other guy and can't stand me in bed anymore and I am so depressed, I am desperate to feel loved and wanted. Every time I reach out to my wife to have sex, even though she reluctantly agrees most of the time, I can tell she is just doing me a favor and she doesn't really want to and she doesn't enjoy it. She wants it over quick. It makes you feel down, man

So, that's why I did it, to boost my ego, to feel loved and wanted. But, you want to know something. It didn't help, it didn't do anything at all, I still feel like shit, I feel so low.

Bartender, two more scotches

Make mine a double."

SHORT STORIES (CONT.)

HURT

One night she and I were making love in her second floor apartment with no light except the dim glow of a distant street light. She was laying on top and moving slowly in rhythm to Jerry Butler's 'Ice on Ice', when she started thinking about Jim again and she started crying, very softly and quietly. I held her tight, never saying a word, until finally she started to tell me about a very naïve young girl, who when she was in high school believed that when two people loved one each other color, race or religion didn't matter. She fell in love with this young white guy and thought he loved her too. He talked about getting married when they finished high school. At first his parents were very polite to her when he would bring her over to his house and never said anything to him, but when they found out that their son was getting serious about a black girl and even talking about marriage, they were shook up and started to do everything they could to stop end it. They told him that if he ever married her that they (the parents, him and the girl) would be ostracized and isolated by the rest of society. Break up with her for her benefit so that you don't ruin her life and then they sent him to Europe for a year right after high school finished.

Left behind was one very sad and deeply hurt young girl.

SHORT STORIES(CONT.)

MEMORIES

I moved down to Pekin, Illinois with my wife and children when I was 29, in 1970 to take a job at Caterpillar. It was in management and was a great opportunity. They had great expectations of me. I was kind of on a one year probation, but after one year they were going to transfer me to another city where there was a law school and would help pay for me to attend the law school.

When we were looking for a place to live, we met this middle-aged couple. She was conservative and religious and they had a house for rent and rented it to us because we were this attractive young couple and I had just gotten that good job at the same place he worked. But my wife and I were not getting along and we didn't spend much time together. My wife at that time was seeing a psychiatrist about the affair she had been having when we were still living in Michigan and maybe it included a new one. Besides that, she also attended a lot of AA meetings and spent a lot of time after the meetings, talking or going to restaurants with people from the meetings. We needed money, so, I took additional part-time job at Sears and that was where I met her, Inez. She was working at Sears. She also modeled clothes for Sears in newspaper ads.

One night, Inez came up to me at work, just before closing and asked if I could give her a ride home and I said "of course", like I would have for anyone. We barely knew one another, we had only talked a few times for a few minutes, but I was very aware of her. She was a tall, slender black girl with legs that didn't stop, and those eyes, wow, big brown eyes. She was very beautiful and I found her to be very desirable. Anyway, to make a long story short that I will tell in another place, we stopped and had coffee and talked for a long time. After that, I drove to a secluded spot and parked, we kissed a lot and had sex and then I took her home. By the time I got home it was very late.

Now I am a very reliable and honest person, someone you count on and trust and I am almost never late. My wife asked me where I had been and I told her, "with another woman" and went to bed. I had to get up very early in the morning for my job at Caterpillar. When I got home from Caterpillar she was not there which was very normal, so I didn't think nothing of it. An hour or two later I got a call from a friend of hers, I had met him once or twice before so I knew who he was. He started talking about how these things work out for the best and other stuff like that until finally it dawned on me that she had left me and three of the kids (Jeff, Steve and Lori) the oldest was 10 years old. No note, no nothing. She had only taken the baby, Erik, the only one that wasn't in school. She had called up her lover in Michigan and he had driven down get her. It turned out that she had been writing letters to him and talking to him every day. To say I was angry, upset and hurt would be an understatement. I was stunned. I shouldn't have been but I was.

After she left, I had to get the kids ready for school and make something to eat for them when they got home from school. So, here I was, a brand new management employee, coming in late and leaving early. I had to get the kids off to school and get home near the time they would get home.

Things I remember. I remember talking and the most quiet musical laugh. She would laugh at all the funny little things I'd say. We never talked about serious things. I remember when she said," I don't even know what you think about politics." It was one of the few times in my life that I didn't know what to say. I don't know why. I know almost everything and have very strong views. I have been studying it since I was fourteen years old. In the fifties, I discovered Ayn Rand and in the sixties, I read everything from the 'John Birch Society' to a great little magazine called 'The Realist'.

Instead, during our few quiet and serious times, we talked of love and hate and living and being alive. I lived in Pekin, Il. (at that time an all white city) and one night near my home we stopped at a grocery store, everything stopped in the store and everyone just stared at us until we left. I would bet that she was the first black person to ever step foot in that store.

She liked children and got along great with mine. As a matter of fact, I marveled at how well. It was the first time I saw the kids go for hours without fighting. She showed them how to draw and drew for them. She would also sit with them and sing. Her voice was beautiful. She could have been a professional singer.

But, I remember one time when she said, "Rod, I don't think I'm strong enough or ready to take care of three children all the time (she was only nineteen at the time). I think that was one of the first times we both realized it wasn't going to work.

I remember walking – we use to walk very fast, holding each other tight, because it was usually very cold.

When people saw us together, it was all stares and looks, especially when we entered a restaurant, almost everyone turned to look at us. Every face mirrored an emotion; hate, disgust, fear, vicarious thrill, envy, etc. One thing it did was make you feel very isolated and together. The two of you against the world.

The first thing that I noticed about her was her eyes. I remember seeing those large dark brown eyes – eyes that saw so deep. Before we ever went out, I would see her watching me, her eyes burning with desire. It would drive me crazy with desire for her. Once we rode an elevator down, alone. Only my extreme cowardice, stopped me from kissing her then and there. She told me, the first time that I was in her apartment, that she had wanted to be with me for some time and when she wanted something bad enough she always gets it and that's when I told her that she was a witch and had cast a spell over me. After that we had a standing joke about her being a witch (wonderful and beautiful), casting a spell.

One night I went to her apartment and after staying for several hours, I decided it was way past time to leave, so I got ready to leave. We kissed and said our goodbyes and she told me to be careful going down the stairs from her second floor apartment, because I'd slipped and almost fell going down that steep narrow circular gothic stairway the first time.

I got outdoors and it was very cold, nineteen degrees below zero. I climbed into the car, but it wouldn't start. The motor slowly turned over about half way and then died. The battery was dead. What to do? I had to get home because the kids were there all alone, but I decided I couldn't think to good when I was freezing to death. So, I jumped out of the car and ran back to the big old house where she lived and climbed those steep narrow curving stairs that reminded me of some movie somewhere. I knocked on her door and she let me in. I told her the car wouldn't start. She said, "Good, you can spend the night here". I told her, "I would love to but I can't leave the kids alone all night". She asked, "What are you going to do?". I told her,

"I don't know, but I might as well be warm while I decide". So, she hugged me tight to warm me up.

First, I called some service stations, but they said that they had so many calls already that it would be Monday before they could get to me and this was on a Saturday night. This was a big problem since I was new in town and knew very few people, so I called the only guy I could think of – my landlord. His wife answered the phone and I told her I was stuck downtown and my car wouldn't start; could he come and pick me up and give me a ride home. She explained that she really doubted it because he was sick and it's late, but that she would ask him. Much to her dismay he said yes.

So, I stood, holding her, while watching out the window waiting for the landlord to come. Finally, I said, "I am going outside and wait for him out there, so I don't miss him, since I only gave him the street corner where the two streets cross and told him to pick me up there". I went to leave, but she stopped me and told me, "I am going out there to wait with you, I am not going to let you freeze to death alone", so I waited for her to get dressed. She pulled on her 'Chukka' boots and put on her white fur cap (the one I always got fuzz off of when I made out with her) and we went out to wait for my ride.

We stood out there in that nineteen degrees below zero weather, stomping our feet, squeezing each other and breathing on each other just to stay alive. I told her, she had to come home with me if my ride ever showed up, because I would have to have her next to me all night long just to thaw out. She laughed and said, "no way", but when my landlord showed up, I opened the door and shoved her in and climbed in alongside her. I did this very fast because it was so cold. As soon as we got in the car I introduced them. My landlord took one look at Inez's dark brown skin and velvety soft brown eyes and it – blew – his – mind. He started driving around stunned -in a state of shock, babbling on about going to some night club and listening to jazz, but then I told him that my friend (Inez) wasn't old enough and that blew his mind too. He was totally unaware that my wife had left me and also inter-racial dating was very rare in that area at that time. So he drove us around showing us where there use to be some bars where they played jazz until they were tore down. I finally told him, can you please take us to my place and when he realized that she was going to be spending the night with me, that also blew his mind. Anyway, when we got to my place he came in with us and we sat around talking (he and I, she just sat there listening). After a little while she started yawning and he said,' I better let you folks get some sleep'. I agreed with him, thanked him for the ride and asked if he would give me a ride back to downtown Peoria tomorrow to get my car. He said that he would be happy to and then we were alone together. Unfortunately, we only got a few hours of sleep because my children woke us up with the noise they made when they woke up. We got up and ate breakfast and I cleaned the house (a real mess) and did the dishes, while she talked to and entertained my children.

About noon, my landlord showed up and she stayed with the children while I went to get the car. That's about it except I had to use ether to start the car and it backfired through the carburetor with a loud noise and flames shooting out, while the hood was up and the landlord was standing right next to it, scaring him half to death. Poor landlord.

ANOTHER SHORT STORY

COUNTING TO 50

My first girlfriend was M.M., because she kissed me on the cheek in school before class when I was hanging up my coat. We were both 11 yrs. Old. My second was Juanita. She was new to my school and very exotic. She was the first Hispanic I had ever seen. A few years later when I was 15 and sixteen I got to know many Hispanic people, because I worked in the blueberry fields, picking blueberries. Maybe she is the reason I seem to have a thing for brown skin. I used to walk her home from school and go over to her house later to play. We were both 12 and we played a game where she would grab my hat and run into her garage to a corner where the light from a street light came through and we could see each other. She would wait there I would grab her and then both of us would wait for me to kiss her but I never did (no guts). We even went to a movie together and It took me more than an hour to get the courage to put my arm around her, but she moved closer to me and made easy for me to hug her. After that, She moved away with her family and so did I. My next girlfriend was Joanne and she was the first girl I kissed. We were both 13 yrs. old. We met at party where we played spin the bottle. I kissed several girls that day. She used to walk me home, because she had several really tough older brothers, big strong guys., so no one ever bothered her. One of them had been in the Marine Corp. and dated my first wife before I met her.

I met her when my younger brother brought her over to meet me with his girlfriend and my car. She was a neighbor of my brothers girlfriend and they brought her over so the four of us could spend the day hanging out together, but the first thing my brother's girlfriend did was pull out some of my poetry (long since lost) from the glove compartment and rave about how good it was, for me it was embarrassing, not because of the content, but because I thought Char(my first wife) would think I was a nerd (I was, but I wanted to be cool, that's why I had traded my plain black Chevy for a baby blue Dodge convertible)

The first woman I had sex with was the young lady who became my first wife and it was in my Aunt Bev's house. They went to work and so the house was empty during the day. My aunt Bev lived way out in the country and had about four horses during this time. I had asked her if it would be alright if I came and rode them sometime and she had said sure. Back then nobody locked their doors in that area. Western Michigan is a beautiful area, was then and still is. So, my girlfriend and I would skip school (high school) and go riding horses at my aunt's farm. The horses would be down by the creek where the grass was higher and thicker. We would go down there and jump on them and ride them back with no saddle or bridle. I would boast her up on to one (she was only 5ft. tall) and then jump up on another by myself. We would put on a bridle at the barn and then take off riding bareback. It was a great place to live and a great time to be alive